WHEN YOU LOSE YOUR JOB

DIFFICULT TIMES SERIES

WHEN YOU LOSE YOUR JOB

DONNA BENNETT

Augsburg

MINNEAPOLIS

WHEN YOU LOSE YOUR JOB

Large-quantity purchases or custom editions of this book are available at a discount from the publisher. For more information, contact the sales department at Augsburg Fortress, Publishers, 1-800-328-4648, or write to: Sales Director, Augsburg Fortress, Publishers, P.O. Box 1209, Minneapolis, MN 55440-1209.

Cover Design by David Meyer
Book Design by Jessica A. Klein

Library of Congress Cataloging-in-Publication Data
Bennett, Donna, 1937-
    When you lose your job / Donna Bennett.
      p.cm. — (Difficult times series)
      ISBN 0-8066-4362-5 (alk. paper)
      1. Unemployment — Psychological aspects. 2. Unemployed — Psychology. 3. Job hunting. I. Title. II. Series.
HD5708 .B445 2002
650.14 — dc21   2001053473

The paper used in this publication meets the minimum requirements of American National Standard for Information Sciences — Permanence of Paper for Printed Library Materials, ANSI Z329.48-1984. ♻ ™

Manufactured in the U.S.A.   AF 9-4362

06   05   04   03   02   1   2   3   4   5   6   7   8   9   10

❧ Contents ❧

❧ Introduction ❧

Losing a job is both a public and a personal event. Every loss is as unique as the situation in which it occurs. Factors such as age, personality, gender, culture, faith, marital status, abilities, values, experience, and education all contribute to the uniqueness of a loss.

In the case of a job loss, as with any loss, you must undergo a period of grieving. This event triggers many thoughts and emotions. While there is no magic formula for handling job loss, this book offers guidelines in five stages to help you recover.

Stage 1: Shock ("I've lost my job!")
Stage 2: Bargaining for answers ("Why me?")
Stage 3: Giving in to reality ("What now?")
Stage 4: Accepting your loss; preparing for
       the future ("What's next?")
Stage 5: Your new job ("I've moved on.")

In recovering from job loss, it is important to recognize and move through each of these stages. Expect to move in and out of the stages of job loss before reaching the last stage. Stage 5 will help you beyond your recovery. It is often overlooked, but can be crucial to your career in the long term.

❧ Chapter One ❧
Shock

Stage 1: "I've lost my job!"
You've lost your job, and you can't believe it.
You are shocked and confused.

Whether you saw it coming, planned for it, or were taken completely by surprise, losing your job can threaten your sense of security, your self-esteem, and even shake your Christian beliefs.

You may have seen the signs: changes in management, talk of a merger or buyout, or rumors of major cost-cutting. Rather than being forewarned, you may have dismissed these as rumblings, for such discussions are part of running just about any business. Maybe you made an assumption—as many do—that hard work, loyalty, and good reviews would make your position secure. Or perhaps you picked up on the clues and decided to put some extra money in savings, just in case.

If you lost your job owing to a company's downward spiral, it was more than likely beyond your control. If the loss resulted from under-performance on your part, it may or may not have been within your control to change things. When unemployment is low, managers are likely to be more flexible about issues such as showing up late or taking a lot of sick days; but on-the-job performance, including attitude, meeting deadlines, quality of work, and so on, is never overlooked, even if it is seldom spoken about. Not all managers are adept at keeping employees informed of unsatisfactory performance.

Whether you were notified specifically or are still wondering if your performance was a factor in your job loss, take this opportunity to evaluate your work values and priorities and see how they measure up to the type of work and environment you want for your future. Your job performance may have suffered owing to your own dissatisfaction.

$\mathcal{A}$ State of Shock

Shock is the first step in grieving a loss. Shock is a reaction to something unexpected that threatens your life or livelihood.

This stage of job loss is often the shortest, yet should not be ignored. Well-meaning friends, co-workers, and family may want to soften the blow with comments such as, "Oh, you'll find another job!" or "You always land on your feet!" On the other hand, you might hear something like, "How could you let that happen?" or "What did you do?" Such comments often indicate another's insecurity. Your loss may have reminded them of the possibility of loss in their own lives. Your friends may be thinking, "If it happened to her, it could happen to me!" Comments from family members may be a result of their fear. They, too, live with the consequences of your job loss.

Try to remember this when you feel you would like more empathy. Friends and family often need to be coached. The best approach is to tell them you need time—time to get used to the fact that you've lost your job. And time to recover. Eventually you will need their help to figure things out. For now, ask them not to dismiss what happened or to place guilt on you. You need a lot of love and support to help you get back on track. Let them know you understand how difficult it may be for them, too.

Security

The cold, hard reality of job loss means the money stops—sometimes right away or within a week or two. If you have severance pay beyond that, it allows you more security as you seek your next job. It also allows you to properly grieve your loss. Ideally, you will have found a new job before your paychecks stop, but that may not be the case. If you are part of a family and are the sole or significant provider, you may worry that you can no longer fulfill your obligation. If you are single, you may have only yourself to consider, yet your obligation to pay your bills still relies on a steady income. Regardless of how your paycheck is needed, loss of security is part of the shock of losing your job.

Self-esteem

When you lose your job, you lose a part of who you are. Your job required time, energy, training, education, skill, and sacrifice. You were hired because your qualifications filled a need. You were part of something bigger—an integral part of a whole system. You belonged. You had purpose and responsibility, all of which are important to a feeling of well-being.

But now you are shocked to discover you have so suddenly become dispensable. Of course, it is not you but your job that is dispensable, even though it doesn't feel that way. Your sense of worth may suffer as a result.

Having a job is a major part of American society and culture. When people meet for the first time, the question most often asked is "What do you do?"

Whatever you do, your job gives you a certain self-image. When that image is taken away, you can feel stripped or even invisible. Right or wrong, you may feel like you no longer matter.

Faith

Mired down in the loss of security and low self worth, everything may seem out of sync—your sense of purpose lost. A feeling of powerlessness prevails. Even strong faith can be questioned at this stage. When you feel you have done all that is expected and are still laid off, you may wonder just what *are* you supposed to think, believe, or do? When you are in shock, your very core is shaken.

WHAT CAN YOU DO?

Grieving the loss of your job is a very important step toward securing your next position. Of course, you might find a job without it, but if you don't properly grieve, it can show up in your attitude and your demeanor. When you allow yourself to grieve, you become familiar with the many feelings and thoughts associated with job loss, and eventually accept those feelings rather than dismiss them as unimportant. If sadness, anger, or bitterness are kept inside or expressed inappropriately, your full energy will not be available to you. You could jeopardize your job search and even your chances of getting the job you want. (Read more about this in chapters 2 and 3.)

The shock stage is usually not the time to take any significant action. You'll need a few days to get used to what has happened. It is difficult to be in shock while on the job, so most employers will suggest that employment be terminated quickly. If you are expected to continue on the job for a period of time, you may want to renegotiate that expectation with your employer. When you are in shock, your performance is likely to suffer, and neither you nor your employer is likely to benefit from such an arrangement.

At the moment of unsolicited change, your routine, your purpose, and your role all shift—reversing any forward movement. Shock is a way for the body to protect itself from overload and from taking in more than it can easily handle. Even if you quickly need to find a way to make money, first give yourself a few days. Take some time to allow yourself to think clearly and to function properly. Rest, exercise, talk to your pastor, friends, or family. Quick-fix or short-term jobs can wait a few days. When in shock, you often just go through the motions, making it possible to sabotage any potential opportunities if you take action too quickly. What you do in the short term may have an effect on your goals in the long term. Take the time to invest in yourself for a few days. (Read more about emotions and short-term jobs in chapter 3.)

Confide in someone close to you—someone who knows you well. Tell them what to expect from you in the first few days. Ask them to let you know if you seem to be in shock longer than is healthy. If that's the case, ask them to encourage you to seek help from your minister or a grief or job counselor.

After the shock wears off, your emotions will begin to escalate (stage 2). How you handle your emotions is key to the strength and long-term effects of your recovery. Whether you stuff your emotions or allow yourself to feel and express them, your reaction can make a difference in the success of your job search campaign—and your life in general during this time of loss.

❧ Chapter Two ❧
Bargaining for Answers

Stage 2: "Why me?"
You question the rationale and bargain
for answers. You deny the truth.

At this stage, the shock is wearing off and the reality that you have lost your job begins to surface. A range of emotions comes in and, at any given time, you might feel angry, sad, fearful, or humiliated—and often, incredulous.

QUESTIONS

You question the rationale behind your loss and bargain for answers. You deny the truth. Friends, peers, co-workers, family—other people you know have lost jobs, but you never thought it would happen to you. Whether the decision to lay you off was business or performance-related, you may try to justify the reasons behind this harsh action. It will seem like a personal affront regardless of the reason. At this stage, as much as you search and bargain for answers, reality often has little insight to offer.

Nothing makes sense as you recount the unfairness of your layoff: you recall many co-workers who seemed less loyal and the extra effort you gave your job. You wonder: how will they manage without you? How will things get done or move forward? What will happen to the project you were working on? How could your boss or your company place so little value on your contributions? Why didn't they ask, you wonder; maybe you could have helped find a solution!

When answers continue to evade you, you may take a new stance and plunge back in memory, searching for things you may have done or failed to do—something you thought went unnoticed or seemed insignificant at the time. "Could it be that time . . . ?" "I wonder if . . . ?" Employers, even when asked why people are let go, will not, or cannot, give direct or specific answers. Laws and privacy concerns force them to be tenuous, evasive, and protective. Even when layoffs are reported in the media, the full story usually cannot be divulged.

In the final analysis, however, whether the cause is related to performance or to downsizing to meet the company's profit projections, the outcome is that you no longer have a job, and you are personally affected.

At this stage, you are likely to keep searching for answers. Creativity feeds on ambiguity—when you don't know the answers, it's easy to make up answers, to fill in the blanks.

You question your skills: "Maybe I'm not as good as I think I am!" "Maybe if I had done *a b c* or *x y z*, I would still have my job!" You wonder if you're good enough to be hired by someone else, if your skills are current, and whether you'll be able to make the same money or enough money to meet your obligations and live the lifestyle you're used to. Finally, you tell yourself you can't let anyone know you've lost your job. It would be too humiliating. People will think you're a failure. You feel overwhelmed and hopeless. You wonder: "How could God let this happen?"

When you can't come up with the answers, it is easy to feel out of control. And lack of control often breeds feelings of two types of anger. First, there is anger turned outward, which manifests in blaming everything external: the company, the president, your supervisor, your co-workers, and sometimes people closest to you for not understanding. Second, there is anger turned inward, when self doubt becomes self blame.

Reality is usually somewhere in the middle. It is, of course, not all their fault, nor is it all yours. And if you believe that God has guided you in the past, consider that to be still true.

Eventually, as you work through this stage, these feelings will ease. Until then, doubt may hold you in its grip as you struggle for the "right" answers. It's human nature to doubt at this stage, in this or any other kind of loss.

What Can You Do?

Start by getting support—spiritual, emotional, financial, and job-search support. Asking for support may be difficult, but try to think of it as an action step. Action is the best motivator for moving past shock and out of the questioning stage. Choose people who will listen and advise you objectively. Those closest to you may have too much invested in you to provide the best support at this time—friends and family may be in a hurry to make things "normal" again. How you proceed at this stage, and at what pace, should depend upon your readiness to proceed and what you have at stake emotionally, relationally, and financially.

It may seem enticing to simply watch for the right job by scanning the want ads and surfing the Internet. But while these are important activities, they are passive, not active.

Rather, the support you need to seek now is the first active step in rebuilding the foundation that crumbled when you lost your job. The lasting strength of any foundation is in the step-by-step process used to secure its base.

The following suggestions outline several types of foundational support: spiritual and emotional, financial, and job-search support. Choose elements that are most suited to you in your specific situation, and follow through on them.

Spiritual and Emotional Support

FAITH

Maybe your faith is waning and God seems non-existent, or maybe you need a reminder that God has not deserted you. If that is true for you, talk to a minister, pastoral counselor, or spiritual director (a person certified to guide people on their faith journeys). Make regular visits until you feel more yourself again and are ready to make career decisions.

THERAPY

See a therapist if you can't shake feelings of sadness or depression (signs to look for: inability to sleep or sleeping too much, overeating or loss of appetite, feelings of despair or hopelessness). It is not uncommon to have situational or short-term depression in times of loss. A therapist can help you understand and work through these feelings and help you come to terms with the reality of your job loss. You may need to learn that it wasn't your or anyone else's fault. You may need help in bringing a sense of order and structure and positive self-worth back into your life.

If anger is a problem, a therapist can help you get to the core of it. Anger is often a mask for deeper feelings, such as rejection or powerlessness. Holding anger in can be just as debilitating as expressing rage or having angry outbursts. Even if you think your anger isn't showing, it will often reveal itself in the form of manipulative behavior. Anger keeps people away, and it can prevent you from being authentic; people and authenticity both need to be in good supply as you work through your loss. If anger was a reason for your job loss, dealing with it now may prevent future problems, both on the job and in personal relationships.

Prayer

Once you come to understand your anger, the desire to change for yourself (not just for others) is the most important step in managing it. Self-talk and prayer can be big factors in making this change. Ask yourself how it benefits or serves you to hang on to angry feelings and ask God to help you let go of feelings that may be harmful or over which you have no power. Ask yourself, "What can I control?" Then take appropriate action. (For example: You can control how you choose to think about your former employer, how you do your job search, and how you plan your future.)

Gratitude

Another good exercise to try: at the end of each day— whether you consider it a good day or a bad day— write down five things you are grateful for, even just the blue sky or an unexpected smile from someone. Positive repetitions can eventually replace the negative, and can help you put things in perspective.

Humor

Many studies show that humor helps people in difficult times—physically, emotionally, mentally, and spiritually. Even if you have to force yourself, take in a comedy show, watch reruns of your favorite sitcoms, play a game with a child. Spend time with a person who can always make you laugh. And laugh at yourself once in awhile. An added benefit—friends and family may be more inclined to support you when you work through your struggle with humor and joy.

Reality Check

Do a reality check by going to a job support group and talking with others about your marketability. It can be extremely helpful to see your skills through the eyes of others—and it can boost your self esteem. Job support groups can often be found at local churches, community centers, or at state-funded Workforce Centers. To find information for the

Workforce Center in your area, call: 1-888-GETJOBS or 1-888-438-5627. You will be prompted to punch in your zip code; then you will be automatically transferred to your local Workforce Center.

In addition to the many services they provide for job searches, Workforce Centers are also a source of information regarding your rights and responsibilities in receiving unemployment pay under federal programs.

Financial Support

Make an appointment with a financial planner to discuss the management of your finances during the period you do not have a salary. Look for people who do not charge a fee for this service. If you have a family and/or spouse, this would be the time to get everyone involved. Getting everyone to work together on this can make a big difference. When the facts about your finances are out in the open and everyone knows what to expect—even if they don't like what they hear—it can help in the long term. When the ambiguity is removed, each person involved has a stronger opportunity to do his or her part, thus restoring a sense of control.

If, rather than re-employment, retirement is a possibility, a financial planner can be a great help both in the short- and long-term. This again will require discussions with your family and/or spouse to make sure everyone is on the same page.

Search Support

For most of you, the biggest question you're facing is wondering where you will find your next job and where you can get the help you need. Knowledge, the saying goes, is power, so gathering information helps you gain control, even in a process that has so many unknowns. The ways in which you can find information about work are varied. They include: temporary (temp) work, employment agencies, contract work, recruiters, advertised positions, unadvertised positions, and career change.

TEMP WORK

If you need to make money immediately, or you want to get right back to work because you feel better working, visit a temp agency. According to a regional manager of temporary agencies, even with layoffs, companies continue to hire temps at all levels of responsibility. Employers look for people to work on projects and to fill other short-term needs. The employer pays the temp agency, and the temp agency in turn pays you. Temp jobs can last a few weeks or several months depending on need—some temp jobs turn into permanent jobs. Temp agencies will often provide benefits while you are under contract with them.

EMPLOYMENT AGENCIES

Employment and placement agencies, like temp agencies, are hired by employers to find people with specific experience and skills to fill specific positions.

The difference is that their goal is to fill permanent positions. The Yellow Pages, the Internet, or word-of-mouth are the best ways to find those that will fit your needs.

CONTRACT WORK

Many companies hire back their laid-off workers on a contract basis. It can be a win-win situation for both you and the company. It can provide you with work and pay while you're looking for another job. By hiring on an as-needed basis, the company benefits by not having to pay FICA, medical insurance premiums, and so on, and by getting experienced people who know the company and who don't need training. You may find contract opportunities in other companies through networking with friends, colleagues, and acquaintances. (Read more about networking in chapter 3.)

RECRUITERS

There are two types of recruiters—those who are retained by employers to fill a very specific need, and those who work to uncover job opportunities on their own. Recruiters can also be a source of help for improving your interview skills and your resume.

ADVERTISED POSITIONS

These are the positions you will find advertised in the classified sections of newspapers and on company Web sites. On the Internet, job listings from employment classifieds of more than seventy-five U.S. newspapers and company Web sites can be found on www.careerbuilder.com. You can find job openings in industry specific publications such as the Chronicle for Non-Profits, in your library, and on Web sites such as www.healthjobsite.com. General job listings can be found on Web sites such as www.monster.com.

Unadvertised Positions

These are positions that are available but are uncovered through networking. Some employers, usually smaller organizations, hesitate to run ads because of the time involved in reviewing resumes and interviewing. They prefer to find new employees by word-of-mouth and by networking with people they know personally, in business, or through organizations such as local chambers of commerce.

Through networking, you can find out about actual job openings, and you can sometimes hear of positions that are under consideration—those that are awaiting results of financial projections and year-end profits, for example, to determine whether or not to hire.

Career Change

If you have the time or desire to seek a career change, see a career counselor. This may be one of the few times you will have such a chance. If you've always dreamed of doing something else, or longed for more satisfaction in your work, a career counselor can administer and interpret career inventories to help you discover other options. The counselor can help you apply the test results to your life in a realistic way and assist you in developing a plan to activate a career change. This type of support may seem frivolous when your focus is to get back into another job quickly. However, this is an option that you can consider at any time.

Career change can be explored while working as well. If you long for a career change after taking stock of your previous job, but don't want to take the time now for such exploration, consider your next job as transitional.

Making a career change may involve volunteering in another field to get experience, returning to school, making less money, or an adjustment in lifestyle. These things take time and planning. But even if you are returning to the workplace, you can continue the process of career exploration. It can all be worked into a master plan and implemented over a pre-determined period of time.

Workforce Centers with dislocated worker programs are another source of career change help. Workforce Centers receive funding from state and federal grants and assist people after job loss. If you qualify, you can receive free training in new skills or take refresher courses through community and technical college programs. You can receive help with your resume and learn how to find jobs on the Internet.

Attend job support groups for information as well as emotional support. You will find them a great place to network with others who are between jobs and who are willing to share information. Some groups bring in speakers who offer topics, such as staying current with the new technologies, resume content, interviewing, and marketing techniques. (Check local churches, community centers, and Workforce Centers.)

Age-Related Issues

Age can be a difficult-to-handle factor in job loss. Like it or not, social and emotional stigmas on age are a reality, and we often project them on ourselves and on our ability to secure a new job.

If your job search is limping along and all of your efforts have been met with rejection, you might worry that you are not experienced enough (too young) or over-experienced (too old) for the current job market. Age is an unspoken issue in job interviews, and you will never know if your age prevented you from getting a job.

You can't control what others think, but you can control how you think about yourself—and how you prepare for the job market. The following suggestions can help strengthen self-esteem, attitude, and energy and, in turn, diminish the impact of age as a negative factor.

- When interviewing, dress appropriately for both your age and the job, pay attention to grooming, and trust that you know your field and speak from that knowledge.

- Live healthfully—exercise, eat well, and get plenty of sleep.

- Involve yourself in activities that use and strengthen your skills.

- Stay connected with people in your field.

- Maintain your spiritual practices (reading, meditation, prayer, journaling).

When your energy, self-worth, and enthusiasm are authentic (that is, how you truly feel about yourself, at least most of the time), age becomes a less important issue. You may find that employers will put less emphasis on your age and greater focus on your qualifications and the strengths you bring to the organization.

⚘

Stage 2 of job loss, the questioning stage, can be handled by analyzing where you are, making a plan for getting support, and taking action that fits for you and your circumstances. The steps we have reviewed can move you out of shock, help elevate your moods, and even restore hope. The next stage will help you stay on track and keep your attitude and energy at appropriate levels.

❧ Chapter Three ❧
Giving in to Reality

Stage 3: "What Now?"
You give in to reality: you've got to find a new
job. Your motivation runs hot and cold.

In the third stage of job loss, you may find yourself impatient, your moods swinging back and forth. You've followed advice, you've read career books, and you feel you've learned the "right" way to find a job. It may seem easier, though, to sit at the computer and search the Internet, read the want ads, or wait for someone to respond to the resumes you've mailed or e-mailed.

If you have a temp job, it may not be bringing in enough money and may seem boring if it's not a job that uses all of your skills. Or you may be hoping the company will hire you, but they're slow to make a decision, much less an offer.

Your family and friends may be questioning you: "So, how's the job search going?" "Have you found a job yet?" "Why is it taking so long?" There are days when you feel like staying in bed, pulling the covers over your head, and telling everyone to go away!

It's easy to feel discouraged at this stage. If you haven't fully worked through feelings of anger or resentment—feelings that are often masks for deeper hurts, such as a sense of powerlessness—now would be a good time to face those feelings. Talk to a counselor or a minister. Anger is a natural feeling, but if it is showing up more often than not, you will want to get to its source. And how does anger show up? It may be in loud outward expressions (yelling, rage), shortness with others (sarcasm, impatience), or it may show up as sadness or depressed moods (silence, withdrawal). Ask those close to you what they notice about you. They may be reluctant to bring it to your attention. Tell them that you want to know when your moods or attitude are negative or seem inappropriate.

Why does this matter?

There are several reasons to face these feelings. Feelings of resentment can be big or small, but unless you get them out, look at them, weigh them, and explore whether they are realistic, they can become a burden that gets heavier with time. This is especially so if finding a new job—or in the case of retirement, finding new ways to be fulfilled—takes longer than you expected.

As we saw in chapter 1, openly recognizing, discussing, and understanding feelings are key elements of grieving. They help you to move on. If you hang on to negative feelings, they serve only to rob you of energy and focus, disallowing your full potential and possibly hindering opportunity.

If you register with a temporary agency, for example, you may decide that because it is a short-term solution it won't be necessary to make an impression, as long as you are qualified for the job. Your attitude, however, will be noticed and recorded by all who encounter you—the receptionist, the interviewer, and so on. Interviewers are quick to pick up on any falseness or negativity in your manner and the way in which you answer questions. If hired, your attitude on the job will be noticed as well, and could make a difference should the temp job have the potential to develop into a permanent position.

It is difficult to appear "up" when your "real job" seems to be eluding you. There is so much that is unknown. Your world is turned around, you're trying to cope, you don't feel quite yourself—yet you are expected to appear at your best.

When you work through difficult feelings and focus your energy on planning and preparing for the future, it can literally open doors for you. You are apt to act differently, take more risks, and plan your time efficiently. You will be more at ease.

WHAT CAN YOU DO?

When things seem to slow down, take stock. Taking action is always the key to getting restarted during a slow period. Maybe you have been going about your job search in a random way.

You may want to regroup and use this time to make your approach more deliberate and organized. Reassess what you have done to date by evaluating what is and is not working in your job search. Consider starting with a job search plan that includes these elements: a personal job description, job market exploration, networking strategies, support systems, time management, and education needs. The following plan can be used for seeking a job or planning a career change (see page 45 for a summary of this plan).

JOB SEARCH PLAN

Personal Job Description

Describe the type of job, type of organization, environment, size, and responsibilities you prefer in your next position. Keep in mind that this is a chance to include criteria that may have been missing in your last position. For example:

- A position in which I can use my ability to interact well with people, use my computer skills, organize systems, design curriculum, and manage projects.

- A small, growing company that is family-friendly and provides a service that helps to better society.

- Like-minded people who work together for a common cause, flexible hours, and an opportunity for career development.

Rewrite your resume, with assistance if necessary, to fit the specifications in your job description. Highlight your industry-related skills (such as accounting, medical, human resources, computers, marketing) and your transferable skills (those skills that apply to most jobs: analytical thinking, communication, decision-making, problem-solving, teamwork, critical thinking, leadership). Describe the ways in which you have used these skills and how they have made a difference or obtained results in your previous positions.

Job Market Exploration

Explore companies and identify those that have jobs that fit your job description. You can get a good feeling for how companies operate, both financially and socially, by reading local business publications (most large cities have magazines and periodicals published for businesses and people in their locale) and publications specific to your own industry. Articles in the business sections of newspapers often feature and track the operations of both high profile and low profile companies and interview the key officers and managers. Look on the Internet for articles that may have been written about companies in your area. Include not only local publications but also national tabloids, journals, and magazines, such as the *Wall Street Journal* and *Fast Company*. Make a list of companies that attract your attention and focus your research on them.

Now you have established a profile: a job description and the type of companies or organizations in which you would like to work. Add to your list by asking your personal and business network for further recommendations based on your profile (see Networking Strategies, below).

This process will facilitate your search by making it more specific. It will also make the networking process more strategic.

Networking Strategies

This step may be difficult—you are asking for help and admitting you don't have a job. However, it's human nature for others to want to help. Try to remember that, if approached by someone in a similar situation, you would do the same.

Networking works best when you tell people specifically how they can help.

- Make a list of everyone you know. Tell them you are looking for a new job. Show them your job description, company profile, your list of potential companies, and a copy of your resume.

- Ask what they know and who they know.

- Tell them you want to build your network of contacts to increase your chances of finding the type of job that will give you the greatest satisfaction.

- Keep a notebook (in a three-ring binder or on the computer) to record and track who you have talked to, what you have learned, any outcomes, and what action is necessary for follow up.

- Write thank-you notes and tune in to ways in which you can reciprocate.

- Keep your network informed of your progress. You don't want someone to assume you no longer need their help until you tell them so.

Support Systems

Find a job support group, preferably one that meets weekly (check local churches, community centers, and Workforce Centers). Support group meetings will add structure to your week and can give you a sense of accountability for your weekly goals. You can attend formally established groups, but you might also check with your church or minister to see if any informal groups have formed to give prayer support. You might also start such a group yourself.

As an alternative, ask a friend to meet with you regularly as a prayer partner and for general support. The sole purpose would be to have a person in your network who is there strictly for support—not to judge or give advice.

Keep friends and family informed of your actions. This will help diffuse anxiety in those who have the most invested in your finding a job, and may decrease the number of inquiries you receive about your progress. Let them know when you are actively networking, attending support groups, sending out resumes, and interviewing. Keep those you see less often informed from time to time as well, and let them know when they can provide specific help. Always thank them for their interest.

Time Management

At the beginning of each week, decide what blocks of time you will devote to your job search, and plan how you will use them. This is a great opportunity to hone your organizational skills. Devise a system that is straightforward, effective, and easy to use.

Build in time for family and friends, exercise and recreation, and volunteer work in your church or community. Regardless of your mood (especially if your motivation is low), sticking to a plan that is devoted to your goals—and also builds in time for yourself and time for others—can help spiritually, emotionally, and physically.

Education Needs

If appropriate and affordable, take classes to increase or refresh your knowledge. For example, additional computer expertise can increase your potential value with employers, as can enhanced communication, management, and financial skills. Such courses are typically available through community and technical colleges.

If you're planning to change careers, upgrade your degree, or seek a first degree, you might want to consider a graduate study program or a technical or community college program. To save costs, take classes as you are able, rather than in sequential terms. A degree or certificate can be earned over any period of time (one, two, or five years) as long as the requirements are met. Rather than letting time and cost overwhelm you, take classes at a pace you can manage. Be sure to look into scholarships and other programs to help with the cost of a program of study.

❧

The key to moving beyond stage 3, then, is to reassess and ensure that your job search is well-organized. Only when you have a plan can you really work that plan.

❧ Chapter Four ❧
Accepting Your Loss

Stage 4: "What's Next?"
You skip ahead a few stages and slide back a few,
but you've accepted your loss and look
to the future.

Stage 4 can be difficult. You have been doing everything you know how to do, including following advice from experts and non-experts and working your plan to fit with who you are and the direction you want to take. You may have applied for and interviewed for jobs that seemed to be a "perfect fit," only to have nothing happen.

At this stage, your old job-loss wounds can open again. It can be reminiscent of the shock of losing your job—you thought you were doing what was expected in exchange for a return on your efforts, only to be injured again with rejection.

If you expect and plan for this stage, it can ease the pain. Employers' timelines will never be in sync with yours. There are many reasons you may not hear back from an employer in the timeframe you expect. There are things going on behind the scenes of which you have no knowledge. Other issues may have come up that needed priority attention. Your resume may be stalled on someone's desk. Decision-makers may be on vacation or they may be reconsidering whether hiring a new person is the best business decision. But you can't control what they do, so focus on yourself and your own actions.

Again, action is the key word. It's important to keep moving forward, repeating the steps you have already taken, yet trying a fresh and creative approach. If you stop to "wait and see"—that is, wait for an employer to respond to your resume, job application, or interview—a window of opportunity may close before you have even had a chance to open it.

*W*HAT CAN YOU DO?

The keys for working through stage 4 are attitude checks, planning, focus, and action.

The first step, as mentioned in chapter 3, is to check your attitude. It will help pave the way for everything else you do.

Stay on a regular schedule by attending a weekly job support group. At any given meeting, one person, whether the speaker or a group member, on any given week may offer something valuable that you wouldn't otherwise have found, e.g., a job tip, a resume tip, a new idea for marketing yourself, or a new name to add to your network.

Don't assume that everyone is tired of listening to you. Those who are would not have signed on to be in your support network. Keeping your regular meeting with a "job-search friend" and receiving timely spiritual boosts from your minister or prayer partner can help keep you engaged in your quest. If theological issues still tug at you, a spiritual director may be of help.

Stick to a daily plan for your job search and follow through. Keep your plan reasonable and within your comfort zone, but build in room to stretch as needed.

Maintain balance in your life. Exercise regularly. This may mean that you walk the dog every day, take a daily run or bike ride, work out at the gym, or even volunteer at Habitat for Humanity. Taking some action everyday is key. In addition to improving your personal well-being, getting out of the house to do other things increases your number of contacts and potential for opportunity.

When you are called for an interview, go prepared. Know what you have to offer in relation to the employer's needs. Don't oversell or undersell your experience and skills. Practice your interviewing skills through role-play. You can get this type of help from job-search classes, at the Workforce Centers, or from a career counselor. Videotape your mock interviews. This may be uncomfortable at first, but it can help you feel more in control when you are faced with the real thing.

When interviewing, remember that you are interviewing the employer as much as the employer is interviewing you. First impressions will make a difference for both of you. Just as the employer is looking for appropriate dress, grooming, manner, professionalism, and so on, you will want to pay attention to the work environment. If possible and appropriate, ask for a tour (for some jobs, the second or third interview may be a better time to ask for a tour). Notice how you are greeted and how co-workers talk to each other. Be aware of people's attitudes. Try to have a sixth sense to the things that matter to you in a new job.

As for the interview itself, keep in mind that an interview is nothing more than discovering whether there is a fit between the employer and the candidate. Think of it as two colleagues discussing the needs of an organization and the qualifications that fit those needs. Learn as much as you can about the company, the job opening, and how your background, skills, and experience fit the position. Such preparation can ease the process and help to remove some of the tension.

ℳ

If you have made the decision to retire, you can follow some of the same steps outlined here, but place your focus on how you want to spend your time and what you want to accomplish outside of the workplace. Consider writing a plan with a personal mission statement and goals for the next phase of your life. A plan can help you to focus and to feel benevolent with yourself and others by including the ways in which you will spend time with family, in volunteer work, in recreation, and, if you choose, time for work.

✂ Chapter Five ✄
Your New Job

Stage 5: "Moving On"
You've accepted a new job.
You relax and let things flow.

You have a new job. You may tell yourself: "I've made it! This time will be different!" But another voice is telling you: "Watch out! It could happen again!"

It is common to heave a big sigh of relief at this stage. Your arduous job search is over. You can stop worrying about the unknown. You can take back your life again.

Granted, you'll feel some anxiety about learning the job and building relationships with new colleagues. Forging new territory can be scary at first. Some will sit back and survey the comings and goings in the new workplace, noticing what is and is not accepted, and paying attention to how things are done. Others will jump right in and vigorously embrace the challenge of the new situation. Regardless of your approach, consider using a segment of the time you spend at work, the time you think about work, and the time you talk about work as preparation for your next job. Begin with the first few months.

During the first few months on the job—the "honeymoon" phase—take a very active approach to your career. Actions you take now can make a difference in your next job transition, whether it is in the same organization or in a new workplace.

What Can You Do?

Ask for clarity regarding expectations. What are your responsibilities? What are the criteria for bonuses, raises, and so on? Each workplace will provide clarity in its own way, but it is best to seek it early. Ask the person to whom you report if you can take a half hour for this purpose. Repeat back what is said and take notes. Say that you will type it up and put it in your file, so you can be sure that you are meeting expectations. Ask for periodic meetings to ensure that you're on track.

Why does it matter?

Taking this action now can set the pace for the future. It's a proactive approach. It can help reduce assumptions and minimize surprises.

❧

Think about improvements you would have liked to have made in your last job. If it's possible to have it in your new job, now is the time to ask for it. For example, if you are assigned a secretary or other administrative support, rather than letting things work out as they will, sit down with that person or persons and talk about your work styles, the workload, and how to work together to achieve the best results. The goal is to create healthy working relationships.

Why does it matter?

Creating and facilitating healthy relationships can help you feel more in charge of your work.

✌

Consider hiring a personal job coach from outside the workplace (check www.coachfederation.org on the Internet for resources and information). In regularly scheduled meetings, by phone, or in person, a job coach can help you work through personality conflicts on the job, help you approach a difficult situation, advise you on how to ask for a raise, bonus, or promotion, or help you prepare for a promotion. Ask about a coach's credentials and experience, and ask for references from colleagues, or, if appropriate, people who have used their services.

Why does it matter?

Taking this step early can help you handle difficult or tenuous situations before they escalate to proportions that seem unresolvable. It can allow you an opportunity to reduce stress or forego a feeling of isolation before things get to a point where you don't want to come to work.

✌

Set boundaries around hours. If you have typically worked a lot of extra hours and want to change that in this job, decide what is reasonable for yourself and what it takes to get the job done, and act accordingly. That is, learn to say "no," or learn to delegate. This is easier to do in the early phase of your job, rather than later, after a precedent has been set. (This is the type of issue you could work on with a job coach.)

The opposite is true when your workload slows down. Granted, you may want to use these periods to catch up, to be more flexible with your hours, or to take a breather. But this can also be an opportunity to volunteer for projects outside the sphere of your own job. Such projects might stretch your skills and offer new challenges. You might also make an additional contribution to the company's bottom line.

If projects aren't available, find other ways to develop your skills. Take skills development classes through your company or take them outside of work hours. Look for volunteer projects in an area of interest or seek additional challenges to expand your abilities.

Why does it matter?

Staying current and proficient in other areas may make a difference when it comes to promotions or when decisions are made for layoffs. While it is true that many such decisions are beyond your control, you will be more prepared for any outcome by staying up to date.

❧

Keep your job search network alive. Let everyone in your network know that you have found a job. Convey to each of them how important it was to your job search to be able to ask for their help. Whether they were directly helpful or not doesn't matter. The contact itself was the important factor. Let them know you will keep in touch, and then follow through. How you follow through will differ in each case. Time will certainly be a factor. For those close to you, you can periodically set up a coffee, breakfast, or lunch date. For others, you can occasionally send a note, an e-mail, or an article or other information in which they have an interest. Remind them of your willingness to reciprocate if and when they need your help.

Why does it matter?

Your network can be helpful to you on the job as well as between jobs. You can share industry-related information, such as a new software program, a continuing education class, new vendors, where to get good temporary help, and so on. Look at networking as a win-win situation. It is much easier to ask for help when you build a reciprocal relationship and keep it active. Healthy networking relationships are respectful and professional and they feature shared values. Networks can be very active at times, and seem almost non-existent when everyone is focused elsewhere. Networks are at their best when members understand how the network operates and are willing to participate accordingly.

❧ Conclusion ❧

Working through the stages of job loss is an active process. As you make your way through them, consider the suggestions contained in this book and apply them to the specific circumstances of your loss. Move forward at a pace that works for you.

If you surround yourself with support—spiritual, emotional, physical, and intellectual—you will be doing a great deal for yourself. Relying on your faith will also be important throughout this journey, especially when you encounter obstacles on the way to success. Remember, too, to maintain faith in yourself—your abilities, your character, and your capacity to persevere through hard times—and to be open to unexpected and new ideas as you work through your loss.

❧ *Job Search Plan* ❧

JOB SEARCH PLAN SUMMARY

Personal Job Description Example

To find a position where I can use my ability to inter-act well with people, use my computer skills, organize systems, design curriculum, and manage projects.

Possible titles: Project Coordinator, Program Coordinator, Training Manager, Project Manager

Company/Organization Example

A small, growing company that is family-friendly (allows flexibility for family-related concerns, i.e., sick children, elderly parents, etc.) and provides a service that helps to better society. A company that values flexible work hours, and that provides an opportunity for career development. The environment would include like-minded people who work together for a common cause.

Possible organizations: A nonprofit that serves the community through programs for the elderly; a family-owned business that provides consulting services to start-up minority owned businesses.

Resume Assistance

Make an appointment with a career counselor or take a resume-writing class to customize your resume to fit your job description and goals.

Ask for input and assistance in relating your transferable skills to your experience and to the next job you want.

Job Market Exploration

Research companies to find those that hire, or may have a need for, the type of job you want. Look for periodicals, tabloids, and magazines that profile local companies. Search for information on the Internet.

Networking Strategies

Make a list of everyone you plan to contact. Set up meetings, get introductions from colleagues and friends. Be specific about how they can help you—to make your time and theirs as productive as possible.

Support Systems

Build support into everything you do, every day.

Time Management

Begin each week with your calendar. Example:

Monday: 8:00 AM to 10:00 AM

Place phone calls to set up networking appointments

12:00 PM

Lunch with former co-worker (networking)

2:00 PM to 3:00 PM

Bike ride

7:00 PM to 9:00 PM

Attend Job Support Group meeting

Education Needs

Take classes to upgrade skills—talk to class advisors at community education centers, send for catalogs (or go to the library) from community colleges, technical schools, etc.

OTHER RESOURCES FROM AUGSBURG

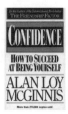

Confidence: How to Succeed at Being Yourself
by Alan Loy McGinnis
189 pages, ISBN 0-8066-2262-8

This book offers practical guidelines to show how you can increase your self-confidence and rid yourself of many negative attitudes.

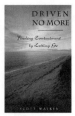

Driven No More: Finding Contentment
by Letting Go
by Scott Walker
126 pages, ISBN 0-8066-4251-3

A clearly written guide for recognizing what is unsatisfying in your life, with a step-by-step guide to choosing the right method of change.

Your Call Is Waiting: How to Recognize
God's Purpose for Your Life
by Terry-Anne Preston
184 pages, ISBN 0-8066-4160-6

Through exploration of Biblical calls, a seven-step discovery method, and a practical activity program, this book will empower you to discern and accept God's calling for your life.

Available wherever books are sold.
To order these books directly, contact:
1-800-328-4648 • www.augsburgfortress.org
Augsburg Fortress, Publishers
P.O. Box 1209, Minneapolis, MN 55440-1209